ITALIAN INFLUENCE ON AMERICAN LITERATURE

An Address by C. WALLER BARRETT and a Catalogue of an Exhibition of Books, Manuscripts and Art showing this influence on American Literature and Art. Held at the Grolier Club, October 17 to December 10, 1961

THE GROLIER CLUB · NEW YORK 1962

Copyright © 1962 by The Grolier Club, New York City

PRINTED IN THE UNITED STATES OF AMERICA

Table of Contents

The Address — *page* 7

The Italian Historical Background — 31

Catalogue of the Exhibition

    LITERARY ITEMS — 37

    SCULPTURE — 56

    PAINTINGS — 57

    DRAWINGS — 61

Plates — 65

Index of Writers and Artists — 129

The Address by C. Waller Barrett

ITALIAN INFLUENCE ON AMERICAN LITERATURE

In 1958, when Van Wyck Brooks sent a copy of his book *The Dream of Arcadia: American Writers and Artists in Italy, 1760–1915*, to Bernard Berenson, Berenson said: "On a lawn in front of the cemetery church at Ferrara there is a beautiful Canovaesque sarcophagus containing the body of a young Bostonian who died there in the eighteen twenties. As a Protestant he could not be buried in holy ground, in the cemetery itself." Berenson was eager to sketch an imaginary portrait of this early pilgrim to the land of his spiritual ancestors. This unknown cultural soldier may well be called a symbol of the feeling that Americans have had for Italy for two hundred years, and he was prophetic of the American writers and artists who have spent their last days on what was to them holy soil. They included Richard Henry Dana, Jr., in Rome, William Wetmore Story in Vallombrosa, and Sinclair Lewis in Florence.

Brooks's *The Dream of Arcadia* is the first general treatment of the theme of American writers in Italy and it is to be hoped that his pioneering effort will be followed by more extended studies. To encourage these further studies is one of the prime objects of this exhibition. The fact that it has been scheduled during the one-hundredth anniversary year of Italian unification provides the opportunity to pay a deserved tribute to Italy for the notable contribution she has made through the years to the development of American literature.

Benjamin Franklin was one of the first Americans to fall under the benign influence of Italian arts and letters. He invented a musical instrument – Franklin's musical glasses – and wrote a friend in Italy that he had derived the name from the Italian; he called it the "armonica." Unfortunately, he never visited the peninsula despite his earnest desire to do so during his ministry to France. Professor Leonard Labaree, editor of the Franklin papers at Yale, tells how Franklin had planned a European trip including Italy in the company of George Washington. This project never materialized but the mind is stirred by a vision of these two shapers of the new American Republic making the grand tour. In any event Franklin learned to read Italian well, became familiar with the literature, and corresponded voluminously with the best Italian minds, scientific and literary. The catalogue of Italian Frankliniana is filled with hundreds of items. An appropriate example is Franklin's *Rules by Which a Great Empire May Be Reduced to a Small One*, a political satire which shows the direct influence of Machiavelli's *The Prince*.

Thomas Jefferson succeeded Franklin at the ministry in Paris. He did achieve "a peep into Eliseum," as he called Italy, and visited Genoa, Turin, and Milan – unfortunately not Rome. His feeling for Italy is shown in his letters to Maria Cosway, the golden-haired Anglo-Florentine wife of Richard Cosway the miniaturist. The buildings of the University of Virginia, abounding in the artifacts of Italian workmen whom Jefferson induced to come to Virginia, are material evidence of the inspiration of Italian architecture.

George Washington never reached Italy, but two of his namesakes – Washington Irving of New York and Washington Allston of Charleston, South Carolina, were more fortunate. In the summer of 1804, Irving traveled from France to Italy, making the final leg in a felucca to Genoa. Irving wrote to a friend that he found a far higher ratio of handsome women in Genoa than in any other city in Europe, with "charming figures, beautiful features and fine black eyes that sparkle with animation or languish bewitchingly – they are as kind too as they are fair and a lover is very rarely known to hang himself in despair at their cruelty." Sixty years later, an "innocent abroad," Mark Twain, said of Genoa: "I would like to remain here. I had rather not go any further. There may be prettier women in Europe, but I doubt it. The population of Genoa is 120,000; two-thirds of these are women, I think, and at least two-thirds of the women are beautiful."

Irving went on: "The innocent familiarities that prevail in America and England are unknown in this country and to press the ruby lips of a fair damsel would be a howling abomination. Such favors are only bestowed by the married lady – in private."

Irving was learning to be a writer by composing long letters and industriously posting his journals. He was also working half of each night on Italian; he had read a translation of *Orlando Furioso* at the age of ten. Irving traveled through Sicily and up to Naples and Rome; and he made a final gallop through Florence. His sightseeing was spasmodic – so thought his brother William who was helping to finance the trip – but his impressions were stored away to provide inspiration later for the Italian sketches in *Tales of a Traveller*.

In Rome Irving visited Canova's studio and found the sculptor at work on the statue of Pauline Bonaparte, the Princess Borghese – in his own words, "naked in the style of the ancients." He met his countryman, Washington Allston, who combined the careers of writer and artist. Allston endeavored to turn Irving's thoughts toward painting but the future author of *The Sketch Book* knew full well the direction of his genius. Allston himself produced *Monaldi*, an Italian Gothic tale of the eighteenth century. His heart, nevertheless, was in painting and he finally settled in Boston to devote the remainder of his life to art. A Charlestonian by birth, he became thoroughly Bostonized, marrying in succession a Channing and a Dana.

In the year 1817, American scholars and historians began to descend on Italy in force. Among them was George Ticknor, who came to study the language and devoted part of his evenings to reading Politian and Alfieri aloud. William Hickling Prescott, later to write his sparkling histories of Spain, Mexico, and Peru, spent six weeks in Rome in 1817. Lord Byron, whose writings had whetted the desire of Americans to see the Pantheon and the Dying Gladiator, became the friend of many of these travelers from the United States. Among others, he met at Leghorn, on an American frigate, a future historian and Secretary of the Navy, George Bancroft, who, in his impetuous haste to tread Italian soil, leaped off the boat and swam two miles to shore. Bancroft, carrying a commission from Lafayette, came to Italy to help the cause of Italian independence.

In 1826, a poet of nineteen departed for Europe to spend three years in preparing himself to teach Romance Languages at Bowdoin College. Henry Wadsworth Longfellow had already visited the peninsula in his imagination and had composed a poem "Italian Scenery" during his junior year at Bowdoin, beginning with these lines:

> "Night rests in beauty on Mont Alto.
> Beneath its shade the beauteous Arno sleeps
> In Vallombrosa's bosom, and dark trees
> Bend with a calm and quiet shadow down
> Upon the beauty of that silent river."

Longfellow traveled overland from Spain to Florence. There he fell prey to a period of listlessness and lack of enthusiasm that caused him to write his mother:

"I got quite out of humour with the language and concluded that I would not give any further attention to speaking – but would make my way through Italy with the little I had acquired and be contented with reading."

When he arrived in Rome, however, he found lodgings on the Piazza Navona with the Persiani family which included three beautiful daughters. These highly educated damsels were able to converse with the budding poet in French and English as well as their native tongue, which, in their mouths, became suddenly beautiful to him. He lingered in this delicious atmosphere, and the knowledge of the Italian language, which had seemed so unimportant in Florence, became imperative in Rome. Then, too, George Washington Greene, Longfellow's great friend, arrived to ramble through Rome and to tell Longfellow about his marathon Italian reading:

"This was my day's round ... I read Dante [in four editions], Tasso's 'Gerusalemme,' the 'Decameron' of Boccaccio, the 'Rime' of Politian, all the tragedies of Alfieri, the principal dramas of Metastasio, – some six volumes, – the 'Storia Pittorica' of Lanzi, the 'Principe' of Machiavelli, the 'Aminta' of Tasso, the 'Pastor Fido' of Guarini, and much of Monti, Pindemonte, Parini, the histories of Botta, the 'Corbaccio' and 'Fiammetta' of Boccaccio."

He also read Manzoni, Petrarch, Guicciardini, Niccolini, Goldoni, Foscolo, etc.

Under these influences Longfellow developed a lifelong devotion to Italian literature which flowered in his translation of *The Divine Comedy*, a poetic one, still believed to be the best in the English language. Longfellow's tribute to Italy in a Harvard lecture of 1851 is an eloquent reflection of his deepest feelings:

"To the imagination, Italy has always been, and always will be, the land of sun, and the land of song; and neither tempest, rain nor snow will ever chill the glow of enthusiasm that the name of Italy excites in every poetic mind. Say what ill of it you may, it still remains to the poet the land of his predilection, to the artist the land of his necessity."

Another poet and philosopher, Ralph Waldo Emerson, toured Sicily and the peninsula. Lonely in Naples and disgusted with the corruption and misery he observed under the Bourbon rule, he paused long enough to write his poem "At Naples." His journal in Rome describes his poor feet – sore with walking all day among the ruins – and follows with this Emersonian poem:

> "Alone in Rome. Why, Rome is lonely too; –
> Besides, you need not be alone; the soul
> Shall have society of its own rank.
> Be great, be true, and all the Scipios,
> The Catos, the wise patriots of Rome,
> Shall flock to you and tarry by your side,
> And comfort you with their high company."

On this visit Emerson spent a month in Florence and saw much of Horatio Greenough, the American sculptor and Fenimore Cooper's protégé.

13

"Greenough's conversation," Emerson said, "was even cunninger than his chisel." Emerson returned to Florence and to Rome in 1873; he was then sixty-nine and no longer lonely but the world-famous author and lecturer.

Emerson was impressed by Milan Cathedral – called it the only church to compare to St. Peter's. He wrote:

"When completed, it will have 7000 statues, great and small, upon the outside; there are now 5000. . . . Neighbored by this army of marble saints and martyrs, with scores of exquisitely sculptured pinnacles rising and flowering all around you, the noble city of Milan beneath, and all the Alps in the horizon, – it is one of the grandest views on earth."

Indeed this cathedral seemed to dazzle Americans. Mark Twain wrote:

"What a wonder it is! So grand, so solemn, so vast! And yet so delicate, so airy, so graceful! A very world of solid weight, and yet it seems in the soft moonlight only a fairy delusion of frostwork that might vanish with a breath! How sharply its pinnacled angles and its wilderness of spires were cut against the sky, and how richly their shadows fell upon its snowy roof! It was a vision! – a miracle! – an anthem sung in stone, a poem wrought in marble!"

Melville was inspired to write the poem "Milan Cathedral" which contains these lines:

> "Of Art the miracles
>   Its tribes of pinnacles
> Gleam like to ice-peaks snowed; and higher,
> Erect upon each airy spire
>   In concourse without end,
> Statues of saints over saints ascend
> Like multitudinous forks of fire."

However, the pragmatic James Fenimore Cooper dismissed it with these words in his journal:

"Leave Sesto at 6. The Country is a vast plain. . . . Got a view of the Cathedral of Milan at the distance of two or three miles. Arrived at 2 – Took a peep at Cathedral, &c."

Cooper left Milan two days later.

and accordingly lived openly with Ossoli. In 1848, she bore him a child; a marriage presumably took place the following year. The advice of the Pole would seem to have been excellent, as a subtle change was observed in Margaret's character. Where in Boston she had been arrogant, loquacious, aggressive, and pedantic, in Rome she became, as Mrs. William Wetmore Story said, "sensitive, confiding, affectionate, generous, and simple." The Ossoli couple fled from Rome in 1849 when the city was taken by French forces and finally sailed from Leghorn for America with their child in May, 1850. The voyage ended tragically when the vessel foundered off Fire Island with the loss of all on board.

Nathaniel Hawthorne, who had known Margaret in Concord, repeated years later in his journal a Roman opinion that the family Ossoli, though technically noble, had really no rank whatever, the elder brother working as a bricklayer and the sisters walking the streets without bonnets – that is, being in the station of peasant girls. Hawthorne went on:

"He, Margaret's Ossoli, was the handsomest man that Mr. Mozier [an American sculptor] ever saw, but entirely ignorant, even of his own language; scarcely able to read at all; destitute of manners – in short, half an idiot, and without any pretension to be a gentleman."

and later:

"There appears to have been a total collapse in poor Margaret, morally and intellectually; and, tragic as her catastrophe was, Providence was, after all, kind in putting her and her clownish husband and their child on board that fated ship."

Hawthorne himself did not arrive in Rome until 1858. He spent days and days exploring the treasures of Rome. He cared little for pictures but was powerfully drawn to the statuary. A note by Hawthorne in his journal is revealing:

"We afterwards went into the sculpture-gallery [at the Capitol], where I looked at the Faun of Praxiteles, and was sensible of a peculiar charm in it; a sylvan beauty and homeliness, friendly and wild at once. The lengthened, but not preposterous ears, and the little tail, which we infer, have an exquisite effect, and make the spectator smile in his very heart. This race of fauns was the most delightful of all that antiquity imagined. It seems to me that a story, with all sorts of fun and pathos in it, might be contrived on the idea of their species having become intermingled with the human race; a family with the faun blood in them, having prolonged itself from the classic era till our own days. The tail might have disappeared, by dint of constant intermarriages with ordinary mortals; but the pretty hairy ears should occasionally reappear in members of the family; and the moral instincts and intellectual characteristics of the faun might be most picturesquely brought out, without detriment to the human interest of the story. Fancy this combination in the person of a young lady!"

Here is the first inspiration for what became the famous *The Marble Faun* published in Boston and London in 1860.

When Napoleon III's troops poured into Rome, Hawthorne's attitude, at first favorable, became somewhat ambivalent. He had discovered that he had a strange affection for the city and he wrote:

"It is very singular, the sad embrace with which Rome takes possession of the soul. . . . We felt the city pulling at our heart strings far more than London did. . . . It may be because the intellect finds a home there more than in any other spot in the world, and wins the heart to stay with it. . . ."

As the abortive and unsuccessful revolts and campaigns of 1848 faded into history, the Italian patriots gathered themselves for the supreme and successful efforts of 1860–61. Henry Adams first arrived in Italy in 1860. Years later he wrote: "The first plunge into Italy passed Beethoven as a piece of accidental education." After passing in Rome what he describes as "the happiest month of May that life had yet offered," Adams writes in his *Education* in the third person:

"He went on to Naples, and there, in the hot June, heard rumors that Garibaldi and his thousand were about to attack Palermo. Calling on the American minister, Chandler of Pennsylvania, he was kindly treated, not for his merit but for his name, and Mr. Chandler amiably consented to send him to the seat of war as bearer of despatches to Captain Palmer of the American sloop of war

'Iroquois.' Young Adams seized the chance, and went to Palermo in a government transport filled with fleas, commanded by a charming Prince Caracciolo....

"Captain Palmer of the 'Iroquois,' who was a friend of the young man's uncle, Sidney Brooks, took him with the officers of the ship to make an evening call on Garibaldi, whom they found in the Senate House towards sunset, at supper with his picturesque and piratic staff, in the full noise and color of the Palermo revolution. As a spectacle, it belonged to Rossini and the Italian Opera, or to Alexander Dumas at the least, but the spectacle was not its educational side. Garibaldi left the table, and, sitting down at the window, had a few words of talk with Captain Palmer and young Adams. At that moment, in the summer of 1860, Garibaldi was certainly the most serious of the doubtful energies in the world; the most essential to gauge rightly....

"Adams had the chance to look this sphinx in the eyes, and, for five minutes to watch him like a wild animal, at the moment of his greatest achievement and most splendid action. One saw a quiet-featured, quiet-voiced man in a red flannel shirt; absolutely impervious; a type of which Adams knew nothing. Sympathetic it was, and one felt that it was simple; one suspected even that it might be childlike, but could form no guess of its intelligence. In his own eyes Garibaldi might be a Napoleon or a Spartacus; in the hands of Cavour he might become a Condottiere; in the eyes of history he might, like the rest of the world, be only the vigorous player in the game he did not understand. The student was none the wiser."

In 1861, William Dean Howells landed in Venice. He was the first in Italy of the triumvirate of writers destined almost literally to divide American literature among them during the remaining decades of the century. All three developed a lasting love for Italy. Following Howells was Mark Twain who arrived with the other "innocents abroad" on the steamship *Quaker City* in 1867 and Henry James who appeared in 1869. Howells had been appointed United States Consul at Venice at a comfortable $1500 a year by President Lincoln in recognition of the campaign biography he had written. H. L. Mencken later called him a draft-dodger. Perhaps a more generous comment would be: *O tempora! O mores!* Before the year was out Howells went up to Liverpool to greet and marry Elinor Mead, sister-in-law of John Mead of the architectural firm of McKim, Mead and White, all three of whom visited Italy and later constructed Renaissance residences, banks, private clubs, and libraries in the United States.

Howells and his newly wed wife found quarters in a palace on the Grand Canal which had been the birthplace of the Doge Marino Faliero. Here Howells sat out the Civil War, immersing himself in the ever-changing scenes that he portrayed in his book *Venetian Life*, which owes its principal charm to the convincing portrayal of ordinary people, tradesmen, street urchins, and gondoliers in their daily rounds.

In 1882, Howells returned to Italy and spent a good part of the year in Florence and traveling through Tuscany with the artist Joseph Pennell, amassing material for *Tuscan Cities*. More importantly he was laying the groundwork for an extraordinarily fine American novel, *Indian Summer*. The *mise en scène* is Florence and, in what has been described as his finest tight-knit Turgenev manner, Howells spun out with consummate art the wry love story of the American journalist, Colville, 41, his contemporary, Mrs. Bowen, 38, and the young Imogene Graham, 19.

Henry James found in Italy the principal scenes for the affecting story of Daisy Miller in the novella of that name and, more importantly, for the ironic tragedy of Isabel Archer in *The Portrait of a Lady*. Poor Daisy – so impetuous, so imperious, so anxious for experiences – in the end, destined by her own obstinacy to sicken and die of Roman fever. And Isabel Archer with her firm resolve to find a nobler and more meaningful life in the Old World than was possible in America – obtusely repulsing the proposals of better men, only to succumb to the specious charm of the odious American expatriate and dilettante, Gilbert Osmond, who almost revels in his flagrant cruelties and deceptions.

Meanwhile James reeled through Italy in a fever of enjoyment. Within a few hours of his arrival he had covered the whole of Rome, visiting St. John Lateran, the Vatican, the Coliseum, St. Peter's, the Pantheon, and the Appian Way. James had come down from what he called "the wholesome tapioca" of Venice and Florence to "the great plum pudding of Rome." At the end of his first day he exclaimed: "At last – for the first time I live."

Although Venice may have been merely wholesome tapioca in James's view, it provided the shadowy and mysterious background for *The Aspern Papers*, that eerie tale of the pursuit of a great American poet's manuscripts.

Two years earlier, an American of a different sort had landed in Genoa to begin his first Italian journey. With a quizzical glance and ever ready to poke fun at the Old World, Mark Twain was in a way the epitome of the American tourist of his period. He had his own convictions and ideas of beauty. He thought the Duomo in Florence one of the finest cathedrals in Europe and St. Mark's ugly. He wrote:

"One's admiration of a perfect thing always grows, never declines; and this is the surest evidence to him that it *is* perfect. St. Mark is perfect. To me it soon grew to be so nobly, so augustly ugly, that it was difficult to stay away from it, even for a little while. Every time its squat domes disappeared from my view, I had a despondent feeling; whenever they reappeared, I felt an honest rapture – I have not known any happier hours than those I daily spent in front of Florian's, looking across the Great Square at it. . . .

"Propped on its long row of low thick-legged columns, its back knobbed with domes, it seemed like a vast warty bug taking a meditative walk."

He greatly admired Titian's famous "Assumption" in Venice but spoke differently of his "Venus" in Florence:

"You enter, and proceed to that most-visited little gallery that exists in the world and there, against the wall, without obstructing rag or leaf, you may look your fill upon the foulest, the vilest, the obscenest picture the world possesses – Titian's Venus. It isn't that she is naked and stretched out on a bed – no, it is the attitude of one of her arms and hand. If I ventured to describe that attitude, there would be a fine howl – but there the Venus lies, for anybody to gloat over that wants to – and there she has a right to lie, for she is a work of art, and Art has its privileges. I saw a young girl stealing furtive glances at her; I saw young men gaze long and absorbedly at her; I saw aged, infirm men hang upon her charms with a pathetic interest. How I should like to describe her – just to see what a holy indignation I could stir up in the world – just to hear the unreflecting average man deliver himself about my grossness and coarseness, and all that. . . .

"There are pictures of nude women which suggest no impure thought – I am well aware of that. I am not railing at such. What I am trying to emphasize is the fact that Titian's Venus is very far from being one of that sort. Without any question it was painted for a bagnio and it was probably refused because it was a trifle too strong. In truth, it is too strong for any place but a public Art Gallery."

As a place to live, Clemens found Italy admirable and in the course of extended visits later on he wrote two well-known works, *Joan of Arc* and *Pudd'nhead Wilson*.

During these years nearly every American writer of consequence visited Italy, and the influence on American writing was far-reaching. However, there were two poets – we might well call them national poets – who, although they never left their native shores, were nevertheless alive to Italian events and influences. Walt Whitman was an inveterate operagoer and heard almost every Italian opera produced in New York. He later remarked that if he had not heard the operas he could never have written *Leaves of Grass*. His paean of praise for Italian music is embodied in his poem "Proud Music of the Spheres."

Our other stay-at-home poet, John Greenleaf Whittier, "friend of man," had a strong interest in the struggle for political liberty in Italy. For his encouragement of the cause he received the personal thanks of Garibaldi. His poems included "The Prisoner of Naples" in 1851 and one called "Rome 1859"; and in the *Atlantic Monthly* of October, 1869, he published the triumphant poetical tribute, "Garibaldi."

And a third American poet who never saw Italy, Edgar Allan Poe, was sufficiently conversant with Italian lore to write *Scenes from Politian*, a play in verse laid in Rome and its environs, one of the characters being Castiglione.

Francis Marion Crawford, son of Thomas Crawford, the American sculptor, was born in 1854 at Bagni di Lucca. He was perhaps the most cosmopolitan of American writers in Italy. Certainly his education was cosmopolitan – he studied at St. Paul's School in Concord, at Harvard, at Trinity College, Cambridge, the University of Heidelberg, and the University of Rome. He spoke or wrote seventeen languages, including Sanskrit. His writing career was a triumphant refutation of the belief that an American novelist must confine himself to the American scene. "Crawford's most significant achievement," writes a discerning critic, Arthur Hobson Quinn, "one in which he has not been surpassed by any writer in English, lies in his novels based on Italian life." The important thing is that he was not merely exposed to Italian life – he really lived it. He dressed as a peasant and for months explored the Abruzzi Mountains and the untraveled parts of Calabria. He saw for himself the ancient castles, the dungeons, the trap doors, and all the apparatus for torture. He ventured into sections that no American had ever before penetrated and where life went on much the same as it had gone on for a thousand years. What is equally important, he also mingled freely with the ruling families, the nobility, and the hierarchy of the church. Therefore, when he composed his famous series of novels about the Saracinesca family, he achieved a versimilitude in background and detail that other writers have sought for in vain.

This nephew of Julia Ward Howe had a career almost as romantic as the lives he portrayed in his fiction. He was a reporter on the *Indian Herald* of Allahabad. In India he became a Catholic convert and he married in Constantinople! Returning to the United States, he wrote for the *Critic* and the *New York World*. In six weeks Crawford composed his first novel *Mister Isaacs*, which brought him immediate renown. He returned to Italy and by 1885 was, like Cooper, established in a sumptuous villa in Sorrento overhanging a cliff with a spacious terrace overlooking the sea. It had a flight of steps that led to a pier, at which was berthed a chartered felucca manned by a disciplined crew, always ready to take him to Ischia, Capri, Sicily, or wherever his fancy dictated. Despite his extraordinary range of interests, Marion Crawford was first and foremost the professional writer – toiling at his desk until his death at fifty-four and producing forty-five novels as well as short stories, historical studies, and miscellaneous works.

Henry Blake Fuller, the Chicago writer, first visited Italy in 1879 at twenty-two and again four years later. Seven years elapsed, however, before nostalgia for his beloved Italy found expression in his first novel *The Chevalier of Pensieri-Vani*, published in Boston in 1890, thus bringing into print one of the most delightful flights of fancy among American writings on Italy. The narrative of the adventures of the young Italian bachelor, the Chevalier, takes us through Pisa, Rome, Florence, Venice, and Siena, under the guidance of a true lover of art. In the book is an American character, Mr. Occident of "Shelby County," thirsty for the best of European culture. Fuller states Mr. Occident's not unprecedented dilemma: "He felt his position one of peculiar hardship. Birth and habit drew him in one direction; culture and aspiration, in another; but he had never been a good American, and he feared he should never make a good European; he was between two fires, both of which scorched him; between two stools, neither of which offered him a comfortable seat; between the two horns of a dilemma, each of which seemed more cruelly sharp than the other."

James Russell Lowell was among the few to recognize the merit of this beguiling work which soon went into a second edition.

Fuller wrote an *Aspern Papers*. His was entitled *A Coal from the Embers*, and concerned two young American writers in Florence working on similar literary projects.

Edith Wharton, too, tried her hand at the theme of *The Aspern Papers* in her story "The Angel at the Grave," but in her version the scene was a Concord-like New England town. Born Edith Newbold Jones in New York in 1862, as a child she learned French, German, and Italian as naturally as she learned English. Her first Italian experiences were in her father's well-stocked library where she read with avidity such books as Hawthorne's *The Marble Faun*, Longfellow's *Dante*, the art commentaries of Anna Jameson, and Kugler's *Handbook of Italian Painting*. On her first visit to Venice and

Florence her father gave her Ruskin's *Stones of Venice* and *Walks in Florence*. Edith's first bit of Italian writing was a poem "The Last Justiniani" published in *Scribner's Magazine* in October, 1889.

In 1902, she published a major work of Italian-American fiction, *The Valley of Decision*, widely acknowledged as the best novel on the eighteenth century in Italy. When queried about the exhaustive studies required to recreate with such fidelity the Italian life of that century, Mrs. Wharton replied:

"The truth is that I have always found it hard to explain that gradual absorption into my pores of a myriad details – details of landscapes, architecture, old furniture, and eighteenth-century portraits, the gossip of contemporary diarists and travellers, all vivified by repeated spring wanderings guided by Goethe and the Chevalier de Brosses, by Goldoni and Gozzi, Arthur Young, Dr. Burney and Ippolito Nievo, out of which the tale grew. I did not travel and look and read with the writing of the book in mind; but my years of intimacy with the Italian eighteenth century gradually and imperceptibly fashioned the tale and compelled me to write it . . . ."

Edith Wharton frequented Italy in the era of the horde of collectors who swarmed over the peninsula to seek out and bring back to America the paintings, sculpture, and bric-a-brac which form the backbone of the holdings of Italian art in American museums and galleries. The forerunners of this acquisitive army were Thomas Jefferson Bryan and James Jackson Jarves. These two perceptive appreciators looked behind the sugared-down versions of the old masters then currently in favor and devoted their attention to the primitives – the pioneers and innovators – rather than to the artists active during and after the Renaissance. Bryan brought his collection back in 1853. Refused house-room in his native Philadelphia, it landed in the New York Historical Society where Henry James saw it and called it "that collection of worm-eaten diptychs and triptychs of angular saints and seraphs, of black Madonnas and obscure Bambinos, of such marked and approved 'primitives' as had never yet been shipped to our shores."

Jarves, too, was ahead of his times. He arrived in Florence in the early fifties and immediately plunged into the substrata of what he called "the world's capital of Bric-a-Bracdom" as if into an inexhaustible mine of old copies and originals. This pioneer had to do his own expertising, as the time was B. B. B. – that is, before Bernard Berenson. As did Bryan in Philadelphia, Jarves tried his collection on Boston; but despite the help of the influential Charles Eliot Norton, his efforts were rebuffed and the collection was finally deposited at Yale as collateral for a loan of $20,000, which has been described as "one of the most irregular pieces of University finance on record and certainly one of the most brilliant." The interest on the loan went unpaid and it was called. At the auction Yale bid in the collection at $22,000, thus consummating one of the greatest bargains in the history of art transactions.

Edith Wharton proved that fiction is stranger than truth when she combined the careers of Bryan and Jarves in the novella *False Dawn*. The hero of this tale, Lewis Raycie, is sent by his New York father to Italy to acquire a gentleman's gallery represented by examples of such highly prized artists as Guido Reni, Carlo Dolci, and the sentimental Domenichino. Lewis falls in with Ruskin. Giotto and his contemporaries become his idols and he attempts to set up in New York a gallery of Christian art. His father disinherits him, calling his cherished works "a pack of bores" with "not a full-blooded female among them." Long after his death, the collection is found in his attic and sold for five million dollars.

Bernard Berenson first visited Italy in 1888, a year after he was graduated from Harvard. Logan Pearsall Smith, Berenson's brother-in-law, said in his reminiscences that there were two intellectuals at Harvard when he was there, Berenson and George Santayana. B.B., as he was later called, preferred the society of his professors to that of the undergraduates, not surprising when we find that his mentors included William James, Charles Eliot Norton, and Barrett Wendell. He also frequented the drawing room of "The Serpent of the Charles," as he called Mrs. Jack Gardner; and later he guided her in the purchase of the collection of Italian masterpieces at Fenway Court in the Isabella Stewart Gardner Museum.

A most unusual investment was made when a group of Berenson's friends put up $750 to send him to Europe for a year. Unfortunately, many of his benefactors kept dropping in on him to observe his progress as their investment, a procedure similar to pulling up a plant by the roots to see how well it is growing. The progress was too slow and the backers were dissatisfied. Mrs. Gardner came to the rescue with a second $750. Berenson repaid this amount and proceeded to help Mrs. Gardner spend $3,000,000 for her collection. Duveen offered $15,000,000 for it, which was refused. From the investment standpoint, the rate of interest on the original loan may be described as satisfactory.

Among Berenson's many accomplishments as art authority or expert, a term he hated, and as brilliant commentator on the Italian scene, the building of one of the richest known art libraries is far from the least. Berenson himself says, and this should be balm to the book collector: "The gathering of these books is the only thing I have accomplished in my life which gives me real satisfaction."

Despite his modest self-appraisal, Il Bibi, as the Florentines called him, became a legendary figure. Americans of all persuasions enjoyed the hospitality of the villa I Tatti in Settignano, that slowly matured monument to civilized taste and discrimination. Among the pilgrims to I Tatti one day were four young men. One was an artist, two ambitious to be art critics. Upon Berenson's query, the fourth young man said he had no interest in art. "Why, then, have you come to see me?" B.B. asked. "Oh, I just thought you were a sight one ought to see" – like the leaning Tower of Pisa.

Berenson was forever amused by the vagaries of tourists. Once in Venice he overheard a French petit-bourgeois husband say with considerable irritation to his wife as they came out of a side street onto the Piazza San Marco: "*I told you* there was a square here." The stories of Berenson are legion. When he was in Venice for the great Bellini Exhibition he met a man whom he had evidently not seen for a long time. They embraced and started a rapid conversation. Soon the man began to cry and moved away. Berenson said to his companions: "That was the director of the museum in Dresden before the war. He returned to resume his former post but the Russians came and carted everything off – all the most beautiful things. What made my friend cry was not alone that they took the things off but that *they were so badly packed.*"

Berenson relates that when Mr. Jack Gardner died, his widow, Isabella, for the first time became aware of money. Obsessed by the fear of losing or spending what she had, she lived thereafter like a starveling in the cheapest hotel rooms, ordering the least expensive meals. When B.B. and his wife were her guests in Boston, the first night at dinner there was scarcely enough to eat. After the theater there was no supper and the Berensons, beset by pangs of hunger, were unable to sleep. They crept downstairs to rifle the icebox and found two dog biscuits.

As the twentieth century wore on, Americans continued to flock to Italy and to write about it. Berenson's contemporary at Harvard, George Santayana, spent the last thirty years of his life in Rome and died there. Born in Spain, of a Spanish mother and father, he mastered many languages but said he was afraid to go back to Spain since he did not speak Spanish very well. World War I inspired Hemingway's *A Farewell to Arms* and World War II, John Hersey's *A Bell for Adano*. F. Scott Fitzgerald, Louis Bromfield, Sinclair Lewis, and later, Tennessee Williams and Truman Capote succumbed to the potent Italian charm. And so, we may be certain, this will continue, so long as Western Civilization endures. We can only breathe a prayer that this glorious country of beauty and tradition, this peninsula which has produced the greatest flowering of creative art in the history of man, this spiritual homeland, this, our Arcadia, be spared the onslaught of the new barbarians.

C. W. B.

The Italian Historical Background

THE ITALIAN HISTORICAL BACKGROUND

Politically and historically the nineteenth century was one of the most important in the annals of the Peninsula as during that century there was realized the ancient dream of a united Italy first envisioned by Dante who was the creator of a common Italian language and culture. Nearly two hundred years later Machiavelli prophesied: "Italy may behold the coming of a savior . . . with what love he would be received in all those provinces which have suffered from the foreign inundations; with what obstinate faith, with what worship, with what fears!" During the nineteenth and twentieth centuries writers and artists from America saw at first hand Italian history in the making. This background is accordingly of great significance in appraising Italian influence on our national literature and the sequence of historical events should be constantly borne in mind to keep the subject in proper perspective.

1815   Napoleon at St. Helena

"Italy . . . surrounded by the Alps and the sea . . . isolated between her natural limits . . . is destined to form a great and powerful nation. Italy is one nation; unity of customs, language and literature must . . . unite her inhabitants under one sole government. And Rome will . . . be chosen by the Italians as their capital."

1815–1831   The Carbonari and the Poets

LORD BYRON 1788–1824: "It is no great matter, supposing that Italy could be liberated, who or what is sacrificed. It is a grand object – the very poetry of politics."

FOSCOLO 1778–1827: "My soul groans for my country, for myself and for thee."

ALFIERI, Conte Vittorio 1749–1803: "Slaves we are now; but at least slaves in roaring anger."

THE ITALIAN HISTORICAL BACKGROUND

1831–1844 Young Italy

MAZZINI, Giuseppe, 1805–1872. Letter to Charles Albert: "Draw a world out of these dispersed elements like a god from chaos; unite into one whole the scattered members, and pronounce the words, 'It is mine, and it is happy.'"

BANDIERA, Attilio (1811?–1844) and his brother Emilio (1819–1844) (Shot at Cosenza): "Tell our countrymen to imitate our example . . . the cause for which we shall have fought and died is the purest and the holiest that ever warmed the heart of man."

1846–1849 The Year of Revolution—Defeat

PIUS IX, 1792–1878 (Pio Nono) becomes pontiff. The People: "We have a Pope! He loves us! He is our father."
The Constitution of 1848.
The year of revolution—defeat.

CHARLES ALBERT: "I abdicate . . . in favor of my son, Victor Emmanuel. There is your king."

NAPOLEON III occupies Rome 1849.

GARIBALDI, 1807–1882: "Fortune, who betrays us today, will smile on us tomorrow. I am going out of Rome. Let those who wish to continue the war against the stronger come with me. I offer neither pay, nor quarters, nor provisions. I offer hunger, thirst, forced marches, battles, and death. Let him who loves his country in heart, and not with his lips only, follow me."

1860–1861 The March of the Thousand—Victory!

Cavour's motto: "Who goes slowly, goes soundly and goes far."
Garibaldi moves on Naples.
The meeting on the waters 1860.
Garibaldi to Victor Emmanuel II: "Hail, King of Italy!"

THE ITALIAN HISTORICAL BACKGROUND

1865–1872   The New Kingdom

The Capital moved from Turin to Florence 1865.
Venice liberated 1867.
Rome evacuated by French 1870 – occupied by Italians.
Becomes Capital 1872.
Victor Emmanuel II: "I have kept my word."

1878–1900   The Dynasty

Death of Victor Emmanuel II 1879 – Accession of Humbert I.
First Ethiopian War – defeat at Adowa 1896.
Victor Emmanuel III becomes King 1900.

1914–1939   World War I – Rise of Mussolini

Italy leaves Triple Alliance and joins Allies.
Versailles – Orlando one of the Big Four.
The March of the Blackshirts on Rome 1922.
Second Ethiopian War 1935.

1940–1946   World War II – The Republic

The tragic alliance with Hitler.
Surrender and death of Mussolini 1944.
Abdication of Victor Emmanuel III 1946.
Humbert II reigns thirty-four days.
The New Constitution and the Italian Republic 1946: "Sovereignty belongs to the people."

Catalogue of the Exhibition

PREFACE TO THE CATALOGUE

The books and manuscripts selected are representative of the tremendous number of literary productions by Americans which give evidence of the Italian influence. An attempt was made to select the works of the most important writers in the field of fiction, poetry, drama and belles-lettres in general. Naturally there are many works which could not be displayed. There are exhibited only a few among the many present-day books which show the continuing strong influence of Italy on the American writer.

CATALOGUE OF LITERARY ITEMS
IN THE EXHIBITION

Benjamin Franklin 1706–1790

1 *Rules by Which a Great Empire May Be Reduced to a Small One.* First page of manuscript. Inspired by Machiavelli's *The Prince.*
2 Plaque by the Italian medalist Giambattista Nini, done from the life in Paris in 1777. Its most distinctive feature is the famous fur cap.
3 Engraving of Franklin. A nineteenth-century Italian engraving designed by G. B. Bosio and engraved by Giovanni Antonio Sasso with the Franklin stove in the background.
4 Aquatint of Franklin. An early nineteenth-century aquatint done by Gallo Gallina, from an engraving by Michele Bisi, after Duplessis.

Thomas Jefferson 1743–1826

5 Letter to Maria Cosway, July 1, 1787. Press copy. Letter from Maria Cosway to Thomas Jefferson, July 9, 1787. Letter to Maria Cosway, September 26, 1788. In his letter of July 1, 1787, to the Anglo-Florentine Mrs. Cosway, Jefferson describes his brief trip to Northern Italy.
6 Jefferson's copy of Piranesi's *Varie Vedute di Roma Antica e Moderna.* Rome, 1748, with binding instructions.
7 Jefferson's original architectural drawings and building instructions for the Rotunda and East Pavilion of the University of Virginia.

Lorenzo Da Ponte 1749–1838

8 "*Un doloroso addio.*" Manuscript of his poem written when the financial crisis of 1831 necessitated the sale of a considerable part of his personal library.
9 *Le Nozze di Figaro.* 1826. First American edition. Da Ponte was librettist for several Mozart operas.

CATALOGUE OF THE EXHIBITION

10 Letter to S. Jarvis, September 12, 1809, describing his teaching at Columbia. Recommends reading Dante, Petrarch, Ariosto, and Tasso.

William Dunlap 1766–1839

11 *Abaellino.* New York, 1802. Translated from the German and adapted for the New York theater.
12 *The Italian Father.* New York, 1810.
13 *Rinaldo Rinaldini.* New York, 1810. Three plays of Italian character. Dunlap was called the American Vasari.

Rembrandt Peale 1778–1860

14 *Notes on Italy.* Philadelphia, 1831. Travel book by the distinguished American painter.

Washington Allston 1779–1843

15 *The Sylphs of the Seasons with Other Poems.* London, 1813. With corrections in the author's hand.
16 *The Sylphs of the Seasons with Other Poems.* Boston, 1813. Includes poems inspired by Italian subjects.
17 *Monaldi.* Published, Boston, 1841; written in Italy, 1822.

Mordecai M. Noah 1785–1851

18 *The Fortress of Sorrento.* New York, 1808.

Henry Pickering 1781–1838

19 *The Ruins of Paestum: and Other Compositions in Verse.* Salem, 1822.

Theodore Lyman 1792–1849

20 *Rambles in Italy in the Years 1816 . . . 17.* Baltimore, 1818. An early account of Italian travel by a Baltimorean.

Washington Irving 1783–1859

21 *Notes of a Tour in Europe 1804-5*. Contains his description of Rome.

22 Letter to Beebe, September 18, 1804. Describes his arrival in Italy (Genoa).

23 *Tales of a Traveller*. Philadelphia, 1824. In four original parts. The sketches in Part III are laid in Italy.

James Fenimore Cooper 1789–1851

24 Manuscript *Journal – Holland and Switzerland, France and Italy*. Cooper describes his arrival at Milan.

25 Letter to Col. R. R. Hunter, Sorrento, September 13, 1829. Writes at great length of his experiences in Italy.

26 *The Wept of Wish-Ton-Wish*. Florence, 1829. 3 vols. Presentation copy to M. Ombrosi, the American consul, who arranged for its printing.

27 *The Bravo*. London, 1831. 3 vols. Original boards. A Venetian story.

28 Volume I of *The Bravo*. Cooper's copy with corrections for a new edition.

29 *The Water-Witch*. Dresden, 1830. 3 vols. Written principally in Sorrento. Cooper tried unsuccessfully to have it printed in Rome; he finally arranged publication in Dresden.

30 *Gleanings in Europe. Italy*. 2 vols. Philadelphia, 1838.

Henry Wadsworth Longfellow 1807–1882

31 Autograph manuscript of Longfellow's translation of *The Divine Comedy*.

32 *The Divine Comedy of Dante Alighieri*. Boston, 1865-7. Volume I of three copies only of the first printing.

33 *Saggi de' novellieri italiani d'ogni secolo*. Boston, 1832. Presentation copy to Rev. Dr. Nichols, Bowdoin College, 1832.

34 *Syllabus de la grammaire italienne*. Boston, 1832. Author's own copy, inscribed to Dr. Bosworth.

35 *Michael Angelo*. London, 1882. In three original parts. Unique Part I, 1882; Parts II and III, 1883.

36 Paolo Ferrari's *Dante a Verona*. Milan, 1862. Printed wrappers. With Longfellow's autograph on front and notation in his hand "From W. S. A. 1866."

Henry David Thoreau 1817–1862

37 Portion of autograph note concerning his efforts to reconstruct details of shipwreck of vessel in which Margaret Fuller was lost with her Italian husband and child.
38 Bachi's *Italian and Spanish Languages*. Boston, 1832. Thoreau's college textbook. With signature in handwriting of his college days, and with a number of words in his autograph.

Edgar Allan Poe 1809–1849

39 *The Raven and Other Poems*. New York, 1845. Contains "Politian," his only play, an Italian tragedy written in 1835.

William Cullen Bryant 1794–1878

40 *Letters of a Traveller*. New York, 1850. Presentation copy to Mrs. L. M. S. Moulton, May 21, 1850. Includes his tour of Italy in 1834.

Henry T. Tuckerman 1813–1871

41 *The Italian Sketch Book*. Philadelphia, 1835.
42 *Isabel; or Sicily, a Pilgrimage*. Philadelphia, 1839.
43 *A Memorial of Horatio Greenough*. New York, 1853.

Ralph Waldo Emerson 1803–1882

44 Autograph manuscript (1843) of Emerson's translation of Dante's *Vita Nuova*.
45 Florence 1576 edition of Boccaccio's *Life of Dante*, Emerson's copy, inscribed by him to S. G. Ward, and by Ward to E. H. Perkins.

Joel Tyler Headley 1813–1897

46 *Letters from Italy.* New York, 1845. Contains "American Artists in Florence."

Sarah Margaret Fuller (Ossoli) 1810–1850

47 Letter to Giuseppe Mazzini. Letter from Mazzini to Margaret Fuller.
48 *At Home and Abroad.* Boston and London, 1846. Presentation copy from the editor, Arthur B. Fuller.
49 *Memoirs.* London, 1852. 3 vols. Posthumous autobiography.

George Stillman Hillard 1808–1879

50 *Six Months in Italy.* Boston, 1853. 2 vols. Hawthorne's close friend and biographer of George Ticknor.

Julia Ward Howe 1819–1910

51 *Passion Flowers.* Boston, 1854. Presentation copy to C. M. Sedgwick. Contains her poem "Rome."

Paul Hamilton Hayne 1830–1886

52 *Avolio; A Legend of the Island of Cos.* Boston, 1860. With presentation slip reading "Richard H. Stoddard, with the affectionate regards of his friend P. H. H."

Nathaniel Hawthorne 1804–1864

53 Holograph French and Italian notebook, February 3-March 10, 1858. Describes life in Rome.
54 Holograph Italian notebook, Rome, March 11-April 22, 1858. Describes first view of "The Faun of Praxiteles."
55 Manuscript diary, Rome, 1859. Describes working on *The Marble Faun.*
56 *The Marble Faun.* Photostat of original manuscript in the British Museum.

57 *The Marble Faun.* Boston, 1860. 2 vols. Presentation copy from Hawthorne's sister.

58 *The Transformation* [*The Marble Faun*]. London, 1860. 3 vols. The Hawthorne family copy.

59 *The Transformation.* Leipzig, 1860. 2 vols. Extra-illustrated.

60 *Passages from the French and Italian Note-books.* 2 vols. London, 1871. Robert Browning's copy.

John Greenleaf Whittier 1807–1892

61 Manuscript of his poem "To Garibaldi."

62 *Miriam.* Boston, 1871. Contains the poem "Garibaldi." Presentation copy to Mary S. Shepard.

63 *The Chapel of the Hermits.* Boston, 1853. Contains the poem "The Prisoners of Naples."

Harriet Beecher Stowe 1811–1896

64 *Agnes of Sorrento.* Boston, 1862.

65 Autograph manuscript of Chapters 20–22, 24–26.

Herman Melville 1819–1891

66 Manuscript of the poem "Milan Cathedral."

67 Manuscript of "Naples in the Time of Bomba" (The Bourbon King Ferdinand).

Thomas W. Parsons 1819–1892

68 Manuscript of his translation of the first ten cantos of Dante's *Inferno*.

69 *The First Ten Cantos of the Inferno* newly translated into English verse. Boston, 1843. Presentation copy to Edward G. Tuckerman.

70 Proofsheets of first published portion. Revisions for Dante's *Inferno*, 1860.

71 *Seventeen Cantos of the Inferno.* Boston, 1865. Presentation copy to Richard Henry Stoddard.

72 *The First Canticle: Inferno*. Boston, 1867. Presentation copy to Howard Ticknor.

James Russell Lowell 1819–1891

73 Autograph notebook with notes on Dante's Beatrice, etc.
74 *Il Pesceballo*. Cambridge, 1862. In Italian by Francis James Child and with English translation by Lowell. First and third issues, one inscribed by Mr. Child. Also Caxton Club edition, 1899.
75 Also: Charles Eliot Norton's copy of the first issue of *Il Pesceballo* with his autograph corrections.
76 *Fireside Travels*. Boston, 1864. Presentation copy to F. J. Child. Contains "Italy."
77 *Among My Books*. Second Series. Boston, 1876. Presentation copy from Charles Eliot Norton to Edward FitzGerald. Contains "Dante."

William Wetmore Story 1819–1895

78 Autobiographical letter to Enrico Nencioni.
79 *Poems*. Boston, 1847. Presentation copy from the poet's wife to T. S. Fay. Contains "Michael Angelo."
80 *Poems*. Boston, 1856. Revised edition. Contains "Italy and New England."
81 *Roba di Roma*. London, 1863. 2 vols. Presentation copy.
82 *Graffiti d'Italia*. New York, Edinburgh and London, 1868.
83 *Vallombrosa*. Edinburgh and London, 1881. Recollections of life at Vallombrosa, where he died in 1895.
84 *Conversations in a Studio*. Boston and New York, 1890. 2 vols. Presentation copy to General Sherman.

Anna Cora Mowatt Ritchie 1819–1870

85 *Fashion*. A comedy in five acts. London, 1850. After a run in New York, Mrs. Ritchie took the play to Florence where it was successfully presented.
86 *Fairy Fingers*. New York, 1865. The scene of part of the novel is in Italy.

J. Bayard Taylor 1825–1878

87 *Rhymes of Travel, Ballads and Other Poems.* New York, 1849. Presentation copy to Thomas Buchanan Read.

88 *A Book of Romances, Lyrics and Songs.* Boston, 1852. Contains "Sicilian Wine."

89 *At Home and Abroad: A Sketch-book of Life, Scenery and Men.* London, 1860. With "Holidays in Switzerland and Italy."

90 *Poems.* Boston, 1866. Presentation copy to Edmund Clarence Stedman with autograph poem, also first draft of sonnet to Stedman.

91 *By-ways of Europe.* New York, 1869. Presentation copy to William Dean Howells.

92 *Views Afoot; or, Europe Seen with Knapsack and Staff.* London, 1869. First English edition; new preface by the author.

93 *Views Afoot.* New York, 1886. Extra-illustrated, including manuscript of Taylor's "Powers' Eve."

C. P. Cranch 1813–1892

94 *The Bird and the Bell, with Other Poems.* Boston, 1875. Presentation copy to William Wetmore Story. Contains "Michael Angelo Buonarroti."

Elizabeth Stedman Kinney 1810–1889

95 *Felicità.* New York, 1855.

96 Journal of her residence in Florence, 1854–56. Writes of her estimate of Hiram Powers.

George Lippard 1822–1854

97 *The Mysteries of Florence.* Philadelphia [1864].

The Lady Annabel. Philadelphia, 1844. Shockers of the period with the scenes laid in Florence.

William Cullen Byrant 1794–1878

98 Autograph letter relating to the meeting for Italian unity held in New York.

Oliver Wendell Holmes 1809–1894

99 *The Unity of Italy*. New York, 1871. Contains letters from Holmes, Whittier, Emerson, Howells, James, and others; a speech by Bryant and a poem by Mrs. Howe.

William Allen Butler 1825–1902

100 *Poems*. Boston, 1871. Presentation copy from the author to Catherine N. Miller. Contains "The Incognita of Raphael."

Charles Dudley Warner 1829–1900

101 *Our Italy*. New York, 1891.

Charles Godfrey Leland 1824–1903

102 *Etruscan Roman Remains*. New York, 1892.
103 *Legends of Florence*. Second Series. New York, 1896.
104 *Arcadia or the Gospel of the Witches*. London, 1899.

Ellen Louise Chandler Moulton 1835–1908

105 *Lazy Tours in Spain and Elsewhere*. Boston, 1896. Contains "Florence the Fair."

James Jackson Jarves 1818–1888

106 *Art Hints*. New York, 1855.
107 *Italian Sights and Papal Principles Seen through American Spectacles*. New York, 1856.

Arthur Sherburne Hardy 1847–1930

108 *Francesca of Rimini*. Philadelphia, 1878. Presentation copy from the author.

CATALOGUE OF THE EXHIBITION

William Dean Howells 1837–1920

109 Manuscript of *Ducal Mantua*. Published in *North American Review*.

110 Manuscript of *Modern Italian Poets*.

111 Manuscript of *Italian Brigandage*.

112 *Venetian Life*. New York, 1866. Presentation copy to James Russell Lowell.

113 *Italian Journeys*. New York, 1867. Presentation copy to Henry James.

114 *A Foregone Conclusion*. Boston, 1875. Presentation copy to Mrs. G. W. C. Noble dated November 28, 1874.

115 *Autobiography. Life of Vittorio Alfieri*. With an essay by Howells. Boston, 1874.

116 *Autobiography. Memoirs of Carlo Goldoni*. With an essay by Howells. Boston, 1877.

117 *Indian Summer*. Edinburgh, 1886. Henry James's copy.

118 *Modern Italian Poets*. New York, 1887.

119 *Venetian Life*. Boston and New York, 1892. 2 vols. Inscribed by Howells; also a signed and inscribed water-color drawing by Childe Hassam, and each plate signed.

120 *Italian Journeys*. Boston and New York, 1901. Illustrated by Joseph Pennell.

121 Translation of *Guide of Venice*. One of two known copies. With Howells' note about his translation of same, signed and dated February 3, 1903.

Henry James 1843–1916

122 Manuscript of "Essay on Venice." Appeared in *Century Magazine*, November, 1882.

123 Manuscript of *Very Modern Rome*. Unpublished.

124 Manuscript of *The Portrait of a Lady*. Revised by James for the New York edition of his works.

125 Manuscript review of Howells' *Italian Journeys*.

126 *Roderick Hudson*. Boston, 1876. Describes experiences of the American artist in Italy. Inspired by William Wetmore Story.

127 *Daisy Miller*, a Study. New York, 1879. Two copies: original printed wrappers; green cloth.

128 *The Portrait of a Lady*. London, 1882. 3 vols. James's own copy.

129 *Daisy Miller*. A Comedy. Boston, 1883.

130 *The Aspern Papers: Louisa Pallant: The Modern Warning*. London, 1888.

131 *Italian Hours*. Boston, 1909. d. j. Illustrated by Joseph Pennell.

Joaquin Miller 1839–1913

132 Manuscript of *Rome*.

133 *The One Fair Woman*. New York, 1876. Mollie Wopsus, according to Miller's family, suggested *Daisy Miller* to Henry James.

134 *Songs of Italy*. Boston, 1878.

Francesca Alexander 1837–1917

135 *The Story of Ida*. Sunnyside, Kent, 1883. Edited with preface by John Ruskin.

136 *Roadside Songs of Tuscany*. Orpinton, Kent, 1884. Published by John Ruskin. With Francesca's letter to Lilly regarding Ruskin's purchase of her book.

Barrett Wendell 1855–1921

137 *The Duchess Emilia*. Boston, 1885. First edition of the author's first book.

F. Marion Crawford 1854–1909

138 Manuscript of *A Lady of Rome*.

139 Manuscript of *A Maid of Venice*.

140 Typescript, with many corrections, and many pages in manuscript of *St. Peter's*.

141 *Saracinesca*. Edinburgh and London, 1887. 3 vols. The first of the Saracinesca series.

142 *With the Immortals.* London, 1888. 2 vols. Dedication copy, inscribed and dated Sorrento, 1888.

143 *Sant' Ilario.* London, 1889. 3 vols. Sequel to *Saracinesca*.

144 *Ave Rosa Immortalis.* New York, 1898. 2 vols.

145 *The Heart of Rome.* London, 1903.

146 *A Lady of Rome.* New York, 1906. d.w.

147 *Address of Marion Crawford.* New York, The Grolier Club, 1904. Catalogue of exhibition of Italian books. One of 306 copies on hand-made paper.

Sylvanus Cobb, Jr. 1823–1887

148 *The Bravo's Secret.* Boston, 1887. Printed wrappers. A Venetian story of the fourteenth century.

Harriet Monroe 1860–1936

149 *Valeria and Other Poems.* Chicago, 1891. One of 300 copies autographed by the author. A play in verse about Italy in the fourteenth century.

Frances Hodgson Burnett 1849–1924

150 *Giovanni.* New York, 1892.

Samuel Langhorne Clemens (Mark Twain) 1835–1910

151 Manuscript of *Pudd'nhead Wilson.* Written in Florence.

152 Manuscript – Chapter XLVII – of *Geneva.* An Italian portion of the manuscript of *A Tramp Abroad.*

153 *The Innocents Abroad.* Hartford, 1869.

154 *A Tramp Abroad.* Hartford, 1880.

155 *The Tragedy of Pudd'nhead Wilson.* Hartford, 1894.

156 *Personal Recollections of Joan of Arc.* New York, 1896. Written in Florence.

George P. A. Healy 1813–1894

157 *Reminiscences of a Portrait Painter.* Chicago, 1894. Describes painting his portrait of Pope Pius IX.

Francis Saltus Saltus 1849–1889

158 *The Bayadere and Other Sonnets.* New York, 1894. Inscribed to J. M. Stoddard.

Constance Fenimore Woolson 1840–1894

159 *The Front Yard and Other Italian Stories.* New York, 1895. d.w.

F. Hopkinson Smith 1838–1915

160 *Well-worn Roads of Spain, Holland and Italy.* Boston, 1887. Inscribed by the author.

161 *Venice of Today.* New York, 1895. Twenty original parts.

162 *Gondola Days.* Boston, 1897. d.w.

Eugene Field 1850–1895

163 *The Love Affairs of a Bibliomaniac.* New York, 1896. Posthumous work. Large-paper edition of 150 numbered copies, with prospectus. Contains "My Romance with Fiammetta."

Ernest Hemingway 1899–1961

164 *A Farewell to Arms.* New York, 1929. Dedication copy. Large-paper edition with bookplate of the dedicatee.

165 *A Farewell to Arms.* First appearance in *Scribner's Magazine*, May-October, 1929. May issue, inscribed under title "In person, his Mark X Ernest Hemingway."

166 Bernard De Voto's review of *A Farewell to Arms* in *Bookwise.* Cambridge, November, 1929.

167 *Across the River and into the Trees.* New York, 1950. One of 25 copies. d.w.

CATALOGUE OF THE EXHIBITION

F. Scott Fitzgerald 1896–1940

168 Manuscript of *Tender Is the Night*. The first page is the first page of the novel as first printed by Scribner's.

169 *Tender Is the Night*. New York, 1934. Printed wrappers. A portion of the novel has a Roman setting.

170 Also presentation copy of *Tender Is the Night* to Joseph Hergesheimer with full-page inscription.

George Santayana 1863–1952

171 Unpublished manuscript: "Ombron and Ambra." Translation of a poem by Lorenzo de' Medici.

172 Manuscript of *Old Age in Italy*. Chapter 7 of Volume III of *Persons and Places (My Host the World)*.

173 *Sonnets and Other Verses*. Cambridge and Chicago, 1894. Two copies; one contains a poem from Lorenzo de' Medici pasted in on the fly-leaf dated June 17, 1896.

174 *Platonism in the Italian Poets*. [Buffalo] 1896. Original printed wrappers.

Henry Blake Fuller 1857–1929

175 Manuscript of *The Chevalier of Pensieri-Vani*. With notebook showing chapter headings.

176 *The Chevalier of Pensieri-Vani*. Boston [1890]. Two copies: gray wrappers and green cloth.

177 Also second edition, presented to J. R. Lowell with A. L. s. to Lowell thanking him for the use of a commendatory letter.

178 *The Last Refuge: A Sicilian Romance*. Boston, 1900.

179 *Waldo Trench and Other Stories of Americans in Italy*. New York, 1908. Presentation copy.

180 *Gardens of This World*. New York, 1929. d.w.

Charles Eliot Norton 1827–1908

181 Manuscript of *Sicilian Journal* with portions by Norton, James Russell Lowell, and others.

182 *Notes of Travel and Study in Italy*. Boston, 1860.

183 *The New Life of Dante Alighieri*. Translated by Norton. Boston, 1867. Presentation copy to Lowell.

184 Proofsheets of Norton's translation of *Dante* annotated by Norton and Lowell.

185 *A Dante Examination Paper*. Harvard, 1897.

Edith Wharton 1862–1937

186 Manuscript of *The Valley of Decision* (portion of).

187 Illustrations for *The Valley of Decision*. Not used.

188 Manuscript of first Italian translation of *The Valley of Decision*.

189 *Crucial Instances*. New York, 1901. Contains two Italian stories, "The Duchess at Prayer" and "The Confessional."

190 *The Valley of Decision*. New York, 1902. 2 vols.

191 *Italian Villas and Their Gardens*. New York, 1904. Illustrated by Maxfield Parrish.

192 *Italian Backgrounds*. New York, 1905.

193 *False Dawn* (*The 'Forties*). New York, 1924. d.w. The first of four volumes of *Old New York*. Composite portrait of Thomas Jefferson Bryan and James Jackson Jarves in the person of Lewis Raycie, a pioneer collector of early Italian art.

Henry Harland 1861–1905

194 *The Cardinal's Snuff-box*. London and New York, 1900. Presentation copy from the author dated May, 1900.

195 *My Friend Prospero*. New York, 1903. Advance copy for private distribution.

CATALOGUE OF THE EXHIBITION

T. A. Daly 1871–1948

196 *Canzoni.* Philadelphia, 1906. The author's first book. Presentation copy to Frank[lin] P. Adams.

Henry Adams 1838–1918

197 *The Education of Henry Adams.* Washington, 1907. Adams's copy with autograph corrections. Describes his meeting with Garibaldi in 1860.

Gertrude Stein 1874–1946

198 *Portrait of Mable Dodge at the Villa Curonia* [1913]. Galileiana edition; limited to 300 copies.

Theodore Dreiser 1871–1945

199 *A Traveller at Forty.* New York, 1914. Presentation copy for Mayan Little. Describes his travels in Italy.

Robert Underwood Johnson 1853–1937

200 *Italian Rhapsody and Other Poems of Italy.* New York, 1918. Presentation copy to Mrs. Goddard.

Edna St. Vincent Millay 1892–1950

201 *Aria da Capo.* New York, 1921. *The Chapbook*, August, 1920. Allan Ross Macdougall's copy.

Sidney Howard 1891–1939

202 *They Knew What They Wanted.* Garden City, 1925. Drama of Italian winegrowers in California.

Thornton N. Wilder 1897–

203 *The Cabala.* New York, 1926. The scene is Rome.

Louis Bromfield 1896–1956

204 *The Strange Case of Miss Annie Spragg.* New York, 1928. d.w. Miss Annie Spragg dies in an Italian palace; her body shows the marks of the stigmata.

Bernard Berenson 1865–1960

205 *Un Antiphonaire avec miniatures par Lippo Vanni.* Paris, 1924.

206 *Venetian Painters.* Final collected edition of Berenson's magnum opus.

207 *The Passionate Sightseer*, from the diaries, 1947–56. New York [1960]. Berenson's last published work.

Sinclair Lewis 1885–1951

208 *Dodsworth.* New York [1928].

209 *Keep out of the Kitchen.* Advance printing, October, 1929, issue of *Cosmopolitan*, inscribed. The scene is Lake Como.

210 Autograph letter from Sinclair Lewis-Bernard Berenson correspondence with photograph of them at I Tatti.

211 Manuscript of *Over the Body of Lucy Jade*, subsequently expanded and published as *World So Wide*.

212 *World So Wide.* New York [1951]. d.w. The scene is Florence.

Mary Austin 1868–1934

213 *Christ in Italy.* New York, 1912. Presentation copy to John O'Hara Cosgrave.

Clinton Scollard 1860–1932

214 *Il Carroccio (The Italian Review).* December, 1916. Contains poem by Scollard, "The Unfading Vision."

Donn Byrne 1889–1928

215 *Messer Marco Polo*. New York, 1921. d.w. Inscribed to James L. Ford.

Thomas Nelson Page 1853–1922

216 *Dante and His Influence*. New York, 1922. Page was American Ambassador to Italy during World War I.

Christopher D. Morley 1890–1957

217 *An Apology for Boccaccio*. Philadelphia, 1923. One of four large-paper copies.

Ezra Pound 1885–

218 Manuscript of *The Pisan Cantos* with changes and additions in the author's hand.
219 Pen-and-ink and wash drawing by Sir Max Beerbohm, signed and dated Rapallo, 1934.
220 *Canzoni*. London, 1911.
221 *Jefferson and/or Mussolini*. London [1935]. "Fascism As I Have Seen It."
222 *Diptych Rome-London*. [Italy, 1957]. One of 200 copies, signed by the author.

Tennessee Williams 1914–

223 *The Roman Spring of Mrs. Stone*. [New York, 1950]. One of 500 copies, signed by the author.
224 *The Rose Tattoo*. [New York, 1951]. A play of the Sicilian colony in the Louisiana bayous.

Robert Nathan 1894–

225 *A Cedar Box*. Indianapolis [1929]. One of 1500 numbered copies.
226 Manuscripts of poems "Como" and "Firenze" included in *A Cedar Box*.

John Hersey 1914–

227 Manuscript of *A Bell for Adano*.
228 *A Bell for Adano*. New York, 1944. d.w.

Harry Brown 1917–

229 *A Walk in the Sun*. New York, 1944. d.w. Novel of one platoon of American soldiers in Italy during World War II.

Edmund Wilson 1895–

230 *Europe without Baedeker – Sketches among the Ruins of Italy, Greece & England*. Garden City, 1947.

Truman Capote 1924–

231 *Local Color*. Melbourne, London, Toronto [cop. 1950]. One of 200 numbered copies. Section on the island of Ischia.

Marcia Davenport

232 *The Constant Image*. New York, 1960. d.w. Presentation copy. A recent "portrait of a lady" – an American in Italy.

Irving Stone 1903–

233 First 25 pages of the final manuscript revision of *The Agony and the Ecstasy*.
234 *The Agony and the Ecstasy*. New York, 1961. d.w. Presentation copy.
235 Italy, where every palace, full of masterpieces, is a masterpiece itself. Folio broadside. The Grabhorn Press, 1937. Only copy known.

CATALOGUE OF SCULPTURE, PAINTINGS, DRAWINGS AND ETCHINGS IN THE EXHIBITION

As background for the exhibition of the works of American writers, there are shown examples of the productions of American artists who studied and worked in Italy during the time when Italian influence on American letters was developing in strength. No artist lives or works in a vacuum, and companionship between the American literary artist and his fellow practitioner in the plastic arts was particularly strong. In some cases the individual artist sought expression in both the literary and the graphic fields, notably: Washington Allston, William Wetmore Story, Thomas Buchanan Read, and James A. McNeill Whistler.

SCULPTURE

236 **Hiram Powers** (1805–1873): Greek Slave – 1843

Born in Vermont, Powers began his career in Cincinnati modeling wax figures for a representation of Dante's *Inferno*. He sailed for Italy in 1837 and remained there for the rest of his life. John Quincy Adams' apostrophe to Hiram Powers reads:

> "Artist! May fortune smile upon thy hand!
> Go forth and rival Greece's art sublime;
> Return, and bid the statesmen of this land
> Live in thy marble for all after-time!"

237 **Horatio Greenough** (1805–1852): Bust of James Fenimore Cooper – 1829

A product of Boston, Greenough studied in Italy from 1824 to 1826. He returned in 1829 and settled in Florence for twenty years. Greenough visited the United States in 1842 to deliver his colossal statue of George Washington. Cooper saw much of him in Florence and became an early patron and supporter.

238 **Horatio Greenough:** Bust of John Quincy Adams

PAINTINGS

239 **Washington Allston (1779–1843): Evening Hymn**

Born in Waccamaw, South Carolina, Allston was in Italy from 1804 to 1808. A dedicated artist, he was also a poet, whose verse was praised by Wordsworth, Southey, and Lowell. In 1841 he published a novel, *Monaldi*, with an Italian setting.

240 **Albert Bierstadt (1830–1902): The Arch of Octavius, Rome – 1855**

In his infancy, Bierstadt was brought from Germany to America and was reared in New Bedford. He is known now principally for his landscapes of Western scenes. Bierstadt spent the winter of 1857–58 in Rome.

241 **George Loring Brown (1814–1889): View of the Campagna and Claudian Aqueduct near Rome**

Brown arrived in Italy in 1840 and remained there for two decades. He became famous for his landscapes of the Italian scene.

242, 243, 244 **Conrad Wise Chapman (1842–1910): Three sketches in oil**

This Virginian fought bravely for the Confederacy. He had spent his youth in Italy and returned there after Lee's surrender in 1865.

245, 246, 247, 248, 249, 250 **John Gadsby Chapman (1808–1889): Etchings colored in oil – water color – etching of the artist in his studio**

Chapman was born in Alexandria, Virginia. He went to Europe in 1827 and studied in Florence and Rome until 1831. Later he returned to Rome and lived there until shortly before his death. His American Drawing Book was published in 1847.

251 **William Merritt Chase (1849–1916): Good Friends –** *circa* **1910**

Chase began his artistic career in his native Indiana. In 1872 he went to Munich and later to Venice where he came under the influence of Tintoretto.

252 **Frederic Edwin Church (1826–1900): Arch of Septimus Severus**

Church was born in Hartford, Connecticut, and studied under Thomas Cole. He established a studio in Rome in 1868–69. Church was one of the earliest collectors of European antique furniture.

253 **Frederic Edwin Church: Between Ceppo Morelli and Ponte Grande**

CATALOGUE OF THE EXHIBITION

254 Frederic Edwin Church: Paestum

255 Frederic Edwin Church: St. Peter's from the Pincio

256 Thomas Cole (1801–1848): The Roman Aqueduct – 1832

> Born in England, Cole became father of the Hudson River School and a founder of the National Academy. He was in Florence in 1831 and had a studio in Rome.

257 Jaspar Francis Cropsey (1823–1900): Landscape with Ruins

> Cropsey was born in Rossville, New York, and went to Italy in 1847. He occupied the old studio of Thomas Cole in Rome and Story's house in Amalfi.

258 Felix Octavius Carr Darley (1822–1888): Italian Boy – water color

> A native Philadelphian, Darley won fame as the illustrator of the works of Washington Irving and James Fenimore Cooper.

259 Arthur Bowen Davies (1862–1928): Italian Hill Town

> As president of the Society of Independent Artists, Davies was instrumental in arranging the 1913 Armory Show. He first worked in Italy in 1893 and died in Florence in 1928.

260 Arthur Bowen Davies: Umbrian Landscape

261 Asher Brown Durand (1796–1886): Roman Head

> Noted principally for his American landscapes, Durand became president of the National Academy. He spent the winter and spring of 1840–41 in Rome and found his subjects among the models accustomed to wait on the Spanish Steps for artists to hire them.

262 George Whiting Flagg (1816–1897): Rebecca

> This nephew of Washington Allston spent three years working and studying in Italy.

263 George Whiting Flagg: The Nun

264 William Graham (1841–1910): A Rainy Day in Venice – 1885

> A Californian by birth, Graham made his way to Italy and devoted many years to painting in Venice, Rome, and Capri.

265 **Thomas Hiram Hotchkiss** (1834–1869): Roman Colosseum – 1868

Hotchkiss was much influenced by Ruskin in his earlier years. He spent a considerable portion of his short life studying and sketching in Florence, the Campagna, Perugia, and Capri. He is buried in Taormina.

266 **Thomas Hiram Hotchkiss:** Scene in Italy – 1865

267 **Thomas Hiram Hotchkiss:** Taormina – 1869

268 **William James Hubard** (1807–1862): Horatio Greenough in His Studio in Florence, 1838–39

Born in Shropshire, England, Hubard was brought to America as a child prodigy in cutting silhouettes. He was encouraged by Gilbert Stuart to become a painter and subsequently moved to Virginia from whence he made two visits to Italy.

269 **George Inness** (1825–1894): Roman Campagna

Inness made four trips to Italy and finally set up a studio on Via Sistina in Rome. His son writes of the family spending a summer at Pieve di Cadore, birthplace of Titian, whom his father thought the greatest colorist that ever lived.

270 **George Inness:** View near Florence

271 **Samuel Finley Breese Morse** (1791–1872): The Chapel of the Virgin at Subiaco

Morse was better known as the inventor of the electric telegraph than as an artist. He studied in London under Benjamin West. Morse went to Rome in 1830 to execute many commissions for paintings given him by Americans. These were mostly for copies of Italian masterpieces.

272 **William Page** (1811–1885): Portrait of Harriet Hosmer (the sculptor) – 1854–57

Born in Albany, Page spent more than ten years in Italy, mainly in Rome. He was president of the National Academy from 1871 to 1873.

273 **Maurice Prendergast** (1861–1924): Venetian Well

Prendergast was brought by his family from St. John's, Newfoundland, his birthplace, to Boston, where he spent his youth. He visited Venice in 1898 and made other trips to Italy in 1909 and 1912.

CATALOGUE OF THE EXHIBITION

274 **Maurice Prendergast:** Piazza di San Marco

275 **Thomas Buchanan Read** (1822–1872): Henry Wadsworth Longfellow – 1869

> Read, a native Pennsylvanian, served during the Civil War on the staff of General Lew Wallace. He achieved fame with his poem "Sheridan's Ride." A great friend of Allston and Longfellow, he returned to Italy after the Civil War to make his home in Florence and Rome until 1872.

276 **John Singer Sargent** (1856–1925): Marble Quarry at Carrara

> Sargent was born in Florence of American parents. He painted extensively in England, France, and the United States as well as in Italy. His greatest fame was earned by his portraits in oil.

277 **John Singer Sargent:** Val d'Aosta, Man Fishing

278 **Frank Hill Smith** (1841–1904): Armenian Pulpit in St. Mark's – 1871

> A noted mural painter, Smith became director of the Museum School of the Museum of Fine Arts, Boston. He studied architecture in his youth.

279 **Cephas Giovanni Thompson** (1809–1888): Nathaniel Hawthorne

> Although the portrait shown is one of the author as a young man, Thompson spent seven years in Italy where he became a close friend of Hawthorne.

280 **Elihu Vedder** (1836–1923): Italian Landscape – 1874

> Sprung from old Dutch Hudson River stock, Vedder began his study of art at twelve. At twenty he went to France and Italy. From 1865 on, he made his home in Rome where he died.

281 **Elihu Vedder:** Roman Girls on the Seashore

282, 283 **James Abbott McNeill Whistler** (1834–1903): Two Venetian Etchings: The Palaces – The Two Doorways

> Born in Lowell, Massachusetts, Whistler entered the United States Military Academy at West Point but left before graduation. After five years in France, he settled permanently in London. Whistler made many visits to Italy and was particularly fascinated by the Venetian scene.

CATALOGUE OF THE EXHIBITION

THE FIRST AMERICAN COLLECTORS

Thomas Jefferson Bryan was a pioneer collector of early Italian art. He brought his collection to the United States in 1853 and attempted to establish a Gallery of Christian Art. The collection was rejected by his native Philadelphia, whereupon Bryan presented it to the New York Historical Society.

284 **Thomas Sully** (1783–1872): Portrait of Thomas Jefferson Bryan

285 **Andrea Mantegna** (1431–1506): The Crucifixion – from the Bryan Collection

286 School of Orcagna: Virgin and Child – triptych – from the Bryan Collection

James Jackson Jarves, born in Boston, became converted to "true art" at the Louvre. As a disciple of Ruskin, he made his way to Florence where he searched for the works of early painters, contemporaries and successors of Giotto. He returned with his collection to Boston but his attempts to establish a gallery were rebuffed. Finally, the collection was deposited at the Yale Art Gallery as collateral for a loan of $20,000. When the loan went unpaid, Yale bid in the collection for $22,000, one of the great art bargains of all time.

287 **Larkin Goldsmith Mead** (1835–1910): Bronze Plaque – Portrait of Jarves

288 Artist unknown: Portrait of Amerigo Vespucci – from the Jarves Collection

DRAWINGS

289 **Thomas Cole:** Temples of Juno, Lucina, and Concordia Agrigentum, Sicily – 1842

290 **Thomas Cole:** Temple of Juno Girgenti, Sicily – *circa* 1842

291 **John William Casilear** (1811–1893): Studies for U. S. currency done in Florence – 1840

A native of New York City, Casilear spent most of his professional life there. He became a prominent banknote designer and member of the National Academy. He made two trips to Italy.

CATALOGUE OF THE EXHIBITION

292 **Jaspar Francis Cropsey:** Villa d'Este, Tivoli – 1848

293 **John Gadsby Chapman:** Raphael at Sixteen

294 **Horatio Greenough:** Figure Study after a Statue by Thorwaldsen – from his Italian Sketch Book of 1830

295, 296, 297 **Joseph Pennell** (1857–1926): Three drawings: A Salute to Friends, Siena – Parading the Horses before the Race – Roman Archway, Arco di Augusto, Rimini

> Reared as a Quaker in Philadelphia, Pennell finally succeeded in entering the art class of Thomas Eakins. He traveled extensively through Italy with Howells and James and illustrated some of their books.

298 **Robert Walter Weir** (1803–1889): Italian Church Interior

> Weir was born in New York City and received his early training from John Wesley Jarvis. In 1824 he went to Italy for three years of study in Florence. He succeeded Charles R. Leslie as instructor of drawing at West Point in 1834.

ACKNOWLEDGMENTS

The Grolier Club wishes to express its deep appreciation to the following individuals and institutions who kindly lent material for the exhibition.

    Addison Gallery of American Art, Andover, Massachusetts
    Alderman Library, University of Virginia
    The American Philosophical Society, Philadelphia
    C. Waller Barrett
    Boston Athenaeum
    Boston Public Library
    Philo C. Calhoun
    Columbia University Libraries
    The Cooper Union Museum
    Detroit Institute of Arts
    Harvard College Library
    John Davis Hatch, Jr.
    The Hirshhorn Collection
    The Houghton Library, Harvard University
    Thomas Jefferson Memorial Collection, University of Virginia
    Kennedy Galleries, Inc.
    Knoedler Galleries
    Lilly Library, University of Indiana
    McGregor Library, University of Virginia
    The Metropolitan Museum of Art
    The Montclair Art Museum
    The Pierpont Morgan Library
    Museum of Fine Arts, Boston
    Museum of the Rhode Island School of Design, Providence
    New York Historical Society
    New York Public Library, Berg Collection
    Princeton University Library
    Irving Stone
    Valentine Museum, Richmond, Virginia
    Edwin Wolfe
    Worcester Art Museum
    Yale University Library

Plates

4 BENJAMIN FRANKLIN

Nineteenth-century Italian aquatint by Gallina.

Lent by American Philosophical Society, Philadelphia, Pennsylvania

7 THOMAS JEFFERSON

Jefferson's drawing of Rotunda, University of Virginia, and building instructions.

Lent by University of Virginia, Charlottesville, Virginia

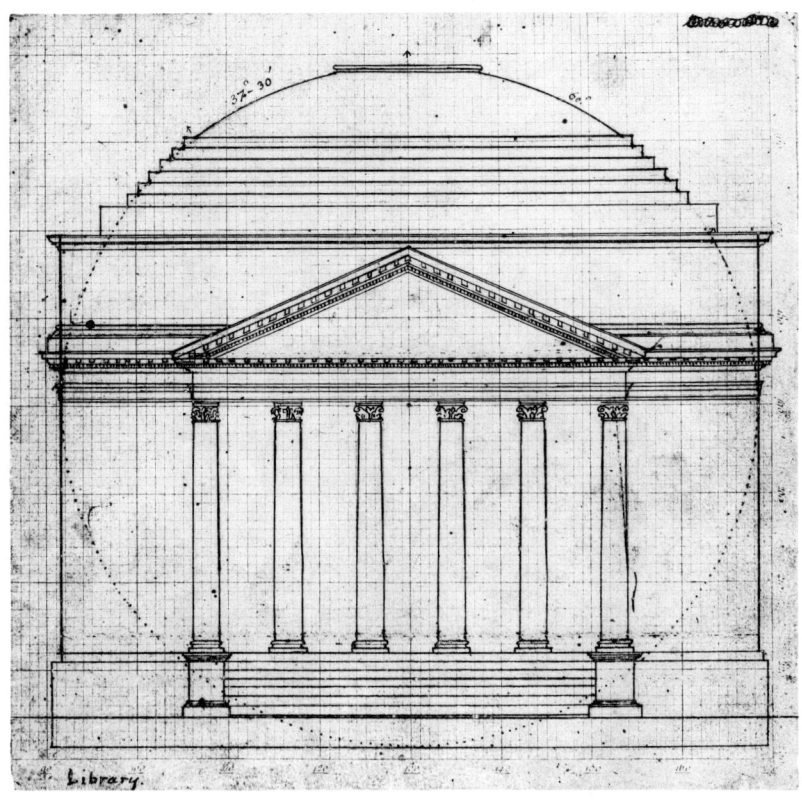

Library.

Rotunda, reduced to the proportions of the Pantheon and accomodated to the purposes of a Library for the University with rooms for drawing, music, examination and other academical purposes.

the diameter of the building 77. feet, being ½ that of the Pantheon, consequently, ¼ it's area, & ⅛ it's volume.
the circumference 242. f.

Library.

8 LORENZO DA PONTE

   Photograph with first page of manuscript poem,
   "*Un doloroso addio.*"

   Lent by Columbia University Libraries, New York, New York

(5) Un doloroso Addio (1)
         a' miei libri.
      Anacreontica

Addio fedeli Amici,
   Delizie del cor mio,
   De' giorni miei felici
   De' rei compagni, Addio.
Vi toglie a me funesta
   Ira d'avverse sorte,
   Una sventura è questa
   Più amara assai che morte.
Il querulo usignuolo
   Cui tolta è la compagna
   D'un disperato duolo
   Non empie la campagna,
Nè Padre mai si duole
   Quando dal patrio lido
   Vede ir sul mar sua prole
   Mentr' ei riman sul lido
Com'io straziar mi sento
   Il cor nel darvi altrui,
   Ch'io perdo in un momento
   Ogni mio bene in vui.
Che per voi sol potei
   Ne' vary umani eventi
   Dar tregua a' mali miei
   Cangiandoli in contenti
E solo a voi Bat'era
   al nome mio dar vita,
   Se rimanessi intera
   La vostra luce unita. (11)

26 JAMES FENIMORE COOPER

The Wept of Wish-Ton-Wish, inscribed "Presented to M. Ombrosi."

Lent by Alderman Library, University of Virginia, Charlottesivlle, Virginia

Presented to Mr Ombrosi
by his Friend
J. Fenimore Cooper

THE WEPT
OF
WISH-TON-WISH

THE WEPT
OF
WISH-TON-WISH
a tale;

BY THE AUTHOR OF THE PIONEERS, PRAIRIE,
ETC. ETC.

"But she is dead to him, to all;
Her lute hangs silent on the wall,
And on the stairs, and at the door,
Her fairy step is heard no more."
Rogers.

VOL. III.

FLORENCE
PRINTED AT DANTE'S HEAD
MDCCCXXIX.

28 JAMES FENIMORE COOPER

The Bravo. Vol. I of Cooper's copy with corrections for a new edition.

Lent by Yale University Library, New Haven, Connecticut

16   THE BRAVO.

the whole of his ~~really~~ fine Grecian face was ~~charged with an~~ expression of coarse humour.

"Look you, Gino—thy master sometimes calls for his gondola between sunset and morning?"

"An owl is not more wakeful than he has been of late. This head of mine has not been on a pillow before the sun has come above the Lido, since the snows melted from Monselice."†

"And when the sun of thy master's countenance sets in his own palazzo, thou hastenest off to the bridge of the Rialto,‡ among the jewellers and butchers, to proclaim the manner in which he passed the night?"

"Diamine! 'Twould be the last night I served the Duca di Sant' Agata were my tongue so limber! The gondolier and the confessor are the two privy councillors of a noble, Master Stefano, with this small difference—that the last only knows what the sinner wishes to reveal, while the first sometimes knows more. I can find a safer, if not a more honest employment,

† [note] The only mountains that rise from the plains of Lombardy. When the vast plain was a gulf, these mountains were probably a high rocky island. They are distant some thirty miles from Venice, on the road to Ferrara.

‡ [note] This celebrated bridge too is divided by two rows of shops, making three passages for those who cross it; the shops that face the inner passages are chiefly occupied by the goldsmiths. Such the stair belongs to the history of Ph. Phillip in the in Canal; the bridge of the Rialto is what which crosses to this island, and into the principal bridge of Venice. The Rialto of Shakespeare was most probably that is Lombardy which was a sort of exchange.

31 HENRY WADSWORTH LONGFELLOW

Manuscript of Longfellow's translation of Dante.
Title-page of *The Inferno* and first page of text.

Lent by The Houghton Library, Harvard University, Cambridge, Massachusetts

The
Divine Comedy
of
Dante Alighieri

Translated by
Henry Wadsworth Longfellow

I have re-read it day by day.
Slow reading so I may the better master.
Menaah

3/05/11

March 14, 1863

Inferno — 1

Midway upon the road of life,
I found myself within a forest dark,
For the straight-forward pathway has been lost.

Ah me! how hard it is to say what was
this savage forest, rough and difficult,
Which in the very thought that renews my fear.

intricate,

So bitter is it, death is little more so;
But of the good to treat, which there I found,
I will tell of the other things I saw there.

I cannot well repeat how there I entered,
So full was I of slumber at the moment
When I abandoned the veracious way.

32 HENRY WADSWORTH LONGFELLOW

The Divine Comedy, showing plate and first page of text (one of three copies only).

Lent by The Pierpont Morgan Library, New York, New York

INFERNO

CANTO I.

MIDWAY upon the journey of our life
 I found myself within a forest dark,
 For the straightforward pathway had been lost.
Ah me! how hard a thing it is to say
 What was this forest savage, rough, and stern,
 Which in the very thought renews the fear.
So bitter is it, death is little more;
 But of the good to treat, which there I found,
 Speak will I of the other things I saw there.
I cannot well repeat how there I entered,
 So full was I of slumber at the moment
 In which I had abandoned the true way.
But after I had reached a mountain's foot,
 At that point where the valley terminated,
 Which had with consternation pierced my heart,

44 RALPH WALDO EMERSON

Manuscript (1843) of translation of Dante's *Vita Nuova*.

Lent by The Houghton Library, Harvard University

6

The New Life of Dante Alighieri.

In that part of the book of my memory before which little can be read, is found this title: *The New Life begins*. Under which title I find written the words which it is my purpose to copy in this book, & if not all, at least their sense.

Nine times since my birth was the heaven of light returned back to the same point in its proper gyration, when to my eyes appeared the gracious lady of my mind who was called Beatrice by many who did not know what else to call her. She had already been so long in this life that in her time the starry heaven was moved toward the point of the East

gentleman to speak with me, to which I, looking on them, answered, asking this glory. And seeing the sovereign in the city, in Beatrice mistress that seemed to the received I cannot say. ... who is say some ... and therefore it annoys, question ... salute you when her ... replied the words that had refuse to the ... truly I know ... you before you have left set a terror .... of wish that

Dante's Vita Nuova
W.M.R.

61 JOHN GREENLEAF WHITTIER

Manuscript of Whittier's poem "To Garibaldi."

Lent by Yale University Library

To Garibaldi.

In trance & dream of old God's prophet saw
  The casting down of thrones. Thou, watching lone
  The hot Sardinian coast-line, hazy-hilled,
  Where, fringing round Caprera's rocky zone
With foam, the slow waves gather & withdraw,
  Behold'st the vision of the seer fulfilled,
  And hear'st the sea-winds burdened with the sound
Of falling chains, as one by one unbound
The nations lift their right hands up & swear
  Their oath of freedom. From the chalk-white wall
Of England, from the black Carpathian range,
  Along the Danube & the Theis, through all
The passes of the Spanish Pyrennes,
  And from the Seine's thronged banks a murmur strange
  And glad floats to thee o'er thy summer seas
On the salt wind that stirs thy whitening hair,—
  The song of Freedom's bloodless victories!

Rejoice, O Garibaldi! Though thy sword
Failed at Rome's gates, and blood seemed vainly poured
  On that red mountain-slope whose ghostly dead,
Unmindful of their murderer's prayer or ban
Walk unappeased the chambered Vatican
  And draw the curtains of Napoleon's bed!
God's providence is not blind, but full of eyes,
It searches all the refuges of lies;
And, in His time & way, the accursed things
  Before whose evil feet thy battle-gage
  Has clashed defiance from hot youth to age
Shall perish. All men shall be priests & kings,—
One royal brotherhood, one church made free
By love which is the law of liberty!

112 WILLIAM DEAN HOWELLS

Venetian Life. Presentation inscription to James Russell Lowell, and title-page.

Lent by Alderman Library, University of Virginia

James Russell Lowell:
"Lu Duca, lu Signore, e lu Maestro."
W.D.H.

VENETIAN LIFE.

VENETIAN LIFE.

BY

WM. D. HOWELLS.

NEW YORK:
HURD & HOUGHTON.
MDCCCLXVI.

127 and 129 HENRY JAMES

Daisy Miller. Two first editions, wrappers and cloth, and first edition of the play.

Lent by Alderman Library, University of Virginia

By the Same Author.

THE SIEGE OF LONDON.

Three Stories in one volume. 12mo. $1.50.

"Full of cleverness, and provokes comparison with some of the best things of Thackeray." — *N. Y. Star.*

"I do not recall a work of fiction for the last year that seems so absolutely indispensable for one to read as this collection. The stories are representative of Mr. James in his best, his most brilliant, and most suggestive work. The fascination of Mr. James is as illusive as light and as all-pervading." — *St. Louis Globe-Democrat.*

"It sparkles with the shrewd, acute speeches, side views into human nature, that gained Mr. James his first popularity. They come upon one unexpectedly, impromptu, a series of fascinating surprises." — *Yale Courant.*

JAMES R. OSGOOD & CO., Boston.

HENRY JAMES

DAISY MILLER

A Comedy

IN THREE ACTS

BOSTON
JAMES R. OSGOOD AND COMPANY
1883

151 SAMUEL LANGHORNE CLEMENS

Manuscript of *Pudd'nhead Wilson*.

Lent by The Pierpont Morgan Library

#6

cise & board in ~~[illeg]~~ Maccaroni & Vermicelli's ~~[illeg]~~ horse-feed shed which is up the back alley as you turn around the corner out of the Piazza del Duomo just beyond the house wh ~~ere~~ that stone that Dante used to sit on, six hundred years ago is let into the wall when he let on to be watching them build Giotto's Campanile & yet always got tired looking as soon as Beatrice passed along on her way to get a chunk of chestnut cake to defend herself with in case of a Ghibelline attack before she got to school, at the same old stand where they sell the same old cake to this day & it is just as light & ~~good as ever~~ good as it was ~~[illeg]~~

165 ERNEST HEMINGWAY

Scribner's Magazine for May-October, 1929. The first appearance of *A Farewell to Arms* inscribed under title for May issue.

Lent by Alderman Library, University of Virginia

SCRIBNER'S MAGAZINE
May 1929

A Farewell to Arms
BY ERNEST HEMINGWAY

THIS is the first novel by Mr. Hemingway since the great success of "The Sun Also Rises." Most of the action takes place on the Italian front during the period of greatest disaster. It is a love-story woven with such a picture of War as would discourage either victors or the conquered from that terrible solution of international troubles.

I

IN the late summer of that year we lived in a house in a village that looked across the river and the plain to the mountains. In the bed of the river there were pebbles and boulders, dry and white in the sun, and the water was clear and swiftly moving and blue in the channels. Troops went by the house and down the road and the dust they raised powdered the leaves of the trees. The trunks of the trees too were dusty and the leaves fell early that year and we saw the troops marching along the road and the dust rising and leaves, stirred by the breeze, falling and the soldiers marching and afterward the road bare and white except for the leaves.

The plain was rich with crops; there were many orchards of fruit trees and beyond the plain the mountains were brown and bare. There was fighting in the mountains and at night we could see the flashes from the artillery. In the dark it was like summer lightning, but the nights were cool and there was not the feeling of a storm coming.

Sometimes in the dark we heard the troops marching under the window and guns going past pulled by motor-tractors. There was much traffic at night and many mules on the roads with boxes of ammunition on each side of their pack-saddles and gray motor trucks that carried men, and other trucks with loads covered with canvas that moved slower in the traffic. There were big guns too that passed in the day drawn by tractors, the long barrels of the guns covered with green branches and green leafy branches and vines laid over the tractors. To the north we could look across a valley and see a forest of chestnut-trees and behind it another mountain on this side of the river. There was fighting for that mountain too, but

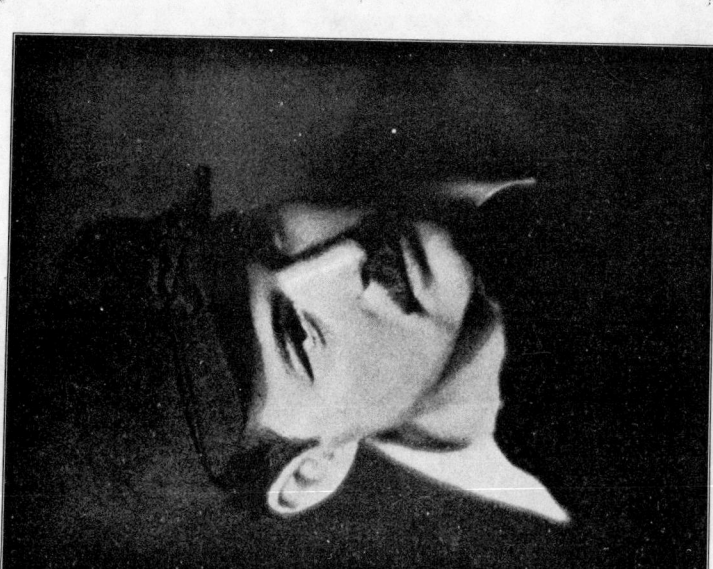

Ernest Hemingway.
From a photograph by Helen Breaker, Paris.

191 EDITH WHARTON

Italian Villas and Their Gardens.

Lent by Alderman Library, University of Virginia

ITALIAN VILLAS AND THEIR GARDENS

BY
EDITH WHARTON

ILLUSTRATED WITH PICTURES BY
MAXFIELD PARRISH
AND BY PHOTOGRAPHS

NEW YORK
THE CENTURY CO.
1904

VILLA CAMPI

210 Photograph of Sinclair Lewis and Bernard Berenson at I Tatti.

Lent by Yale University Library

219 EZRA POUND

Pen-and-ink and wash drawing by Sir Max Beerbohm.

Lent by Alderman Library, University of Virginia

236 HIRAM POWERS

"Greek Slave."

Lent by Knoedler Galleries, New York, New York

237 HORATIO GREENOUGH

Bust of James Fenimore Cooper.

Lent by The Boston Public Library, Boston, Massachusetts

239 WASHINGTON ALLSTON

"Evening Hymn."

Lent by The Montclair Art Museum, Montclair, New Jersey

240 ALBERT BIERSTADT

"The Arch of Octavius, Rome."

Lent by Boston Athenaeum, Boston, Massachusetts

268 WILLIAM JAMES HUBARD

"Horatio Greenough in His Studio in Florence."

Lent by Valentine Museum, Richmond, Virginia

270 GEORGE INNESS

"View near Florence."

Lent by Museum of Fine Arts, Boston, Massachusetts

271 SAMUEL F. B. MORSE

Sketch for "The Chapel of the Virgin at Subiaco."

Lent by Worcester Art Museum, Worcester, Massachusetts

275 THOMAS BUCHANAN READ

"Henry Wadsworth Longfellow."

Lent by The Grolier Club, New York, New York

276 JOHN SINGER SARGENT
"Marble Quarry at Carrara."

Lent by The Metropolitan Museum of Art, New York, New York

279 CEPHAS GIOVANNI THOMPSON

"Nathaniel Hawthorne."

Lent by The Grolier Club

281 ELIHU VEDDER

"Roman Girls on the Seashore."

Lent by The Metropolitan Museum of Art

284 THOMAS SULLY
Portrait of Thomas Jefferson Bryan.

Lent by New York Historical Society, New York, New York

285 ANDREA MANTEGNA

"The Crucifixion" – from the Bryan Collection.

Lent by New York Historical Society

287 LARKIN GOLDSMITH MEAD

Bronze plaque. Portrait of James Jackson Jarves.

Lent by Yale University Art Gallery, New Haven, Connecticut

288 ARTIST UNKNOWN

Portrait of Amerigo Vespucci – from the Jarves Collection.

Lent by Yale University Art Gallery

INDEX TO WRITERS AND ARTISTS IN THE EXHIBITION

	PAGE		PAGE
Adams, Henry	52	Cranch, C. P.	44
Alexander, Francesca	47	Crawford, F. Marion	47
Allston, Washington	38, 57	Cropsey, Jaspar Francis	58, 62
Austin, Mary	53	Daly, T. A.	52
Berenson, Bernard	53	Da Ponte, Lorenzo	37
Bierstadt, Albert	57	Darley, Felix Octavius Carr	58
Bromfield, Louis	53	Davenport, Marcia	55
Brown, George Loring	57	Davies, Arthur Bowen	58
Brown, Harry	55	Dreiser, Theodore	52
Bryan, Thomas Jefferson	61	Dunlap, William	38
Bryant, William Cullen	40, 44	Durand, Asher Brown	58
Burnett, Frances Hodgson	48	Emerson, Ralph Waldo	40
Butler, William Allen	45	Field, Eugene	49
Byrne, Donn	54	Fitzgerald, F. Scott	50
Capote, Truman	55	Flagg, George Whiting	58
Casilear, John William	61	Franklin, Benjamin	37
Chapman, Conrad Wise	57	Fuller, Henry Blake	50
Chapman, John Gadsby	57, 62	Fuller, Sarah Margaret	41
Chase, William Merritt	57	Graham, William	58
Church, Frederic Edwin	57, 58	Greenough, Horatio	56, 62
Clemens, Samuel Langhorne	48	Hardy, Arthur Sherburne	45
Cobb, Sylvanus, Jr.	48	Harland, Henry	51
Cole, Thomas	58, 61	Hawthorne, Nathaniel	41
Cooper, James Fenimore	39	Hayne, Paul Hamilton	41

INDEX TO WRITERS AND ARTISTS IN THE EXHIBITION

	PAGE		PAGE
Headley, Joel Tyler	41	Miller, Joaquin	47
Healy, George P. A.	49	Monroe, Harriet	48
Hemingway, Ernest	49	Morley, Christopher D.	54
Hersey, John	55	Morse, Samuel Finley Breese	59
Hillard, George Stillman	41	Moulton, Ellen Louise Chandler	45
Holmes, Oliver Wendell	45	Nathan, Robert	54
Hotchkiss, Thomas Hiram	59	Noah, Mordecai M.	38
Howard, Sidney	52	Norton, Charles Eliot	51
Howe, Julia Ward	41	Page, Thomas Nelson	54
Howells, William Dean	46	Page, William	59
Hubard, William James	59	Parsons, Thomas W.	42
Inness, George	59	Peale, Rembrandt	38
Irving, Washington	39	Pennell, Joseph	62
James, Henry	46	Pickering, Henry	38
Jarves, James Jackson	45, 61	Poe, Edgar Allan	40
Jefferson, Thomas	37	Pound, Ezra	54
Johnson, Robert Underwood	52	Powers, Hiram	56
Kinney, Elizabeth Stedman	44	Prendergast, Maurice	59, 60
Leland, Charles Godfrey	45	Read, Thomas Buchanan	60
Lewis, Sinclair	53	Ritchie, Anna Cora Mowatt	43
Lippard, George	44	Saltus, Francis Saltus	49
Longfellow, Henry Wadsworth	39	Santayana, George	50
Lowell, James Russell	43	Sargent, John Singer	60
Lyman, Theodore	38	Scollard, Clinton	53
Mantegna, Andrea	61	Smith, Frank Hill	60
Mead, Larkin Goldsmith	61	Smith, F. Hopkinson	49
Melville, Herman	42	Stein, Gertrude	52
Millay, Edna St. Vincent	52	Stone, Irving	55

INDEX TO WRITERS AND ARTISTS IN THE EXHIBITION

	PAGE		PAGE
Story, William Wetmore	43	Weir, Robert Walter	62
Stowe, Harriet Beecher	42	Wendell, Barrett	47
Sully, Thomas	61	Wharton, Edith	51
Taylor, J. Bayard	44	Whistler, James Abbott McNeill	60
Thompson, Cephas Giovanni	60	Whittier, John Greenleaf	42
Thoreau, Henry David	40	Wilder, Thornton N.	52
Tuckerman, Henry T.	40	Williams, Tennessee	54
Vedder, Elihu	60	Wilson, Edmund	55
Warner, Charles Dudley	45	Woolson, Constance Fenimore	49

THE COMMITTEE ON PUBLICATIONS

OF THE GROLIER CLUB certifies that this

copy is one of an edition of 850 copies of which

100 copies are bound with leather back, not for sale,

and 750 copies in cloth. The plates were printed at

the Meriden Gravure Company. The book has been

designed and the text printed at the Spiral Press,

New York. Binding by the Russell-Rutter Company.

Completed in April of 1962

WITHDRAWN